Dr. Alicia Holland's
EXPANDING YOUR TUTORING BUSINESS:
The Blueprint for Protecting Your Learning Organization
2nd Edition

Expanding Your Tutoring Business:
The Blueprint for Protecting Your Learning Organization
2nd Edition

Dr. Alicia Holland, EdD

No parts of this book may be used or reproduced by any means, graphic, electronic, or mechanical, including photocopying, recording, taping or by any information storage retrieval system without the written permission of the author except in the case of brief quotations embodied in critical articles and reviews.

This book may be ordered through booksellers or by contacting:
iGlobal Educational Services, LLC
PO Box 94224
Phoenix, AZ 85070
www.iglobaleducation.com
512-761-5898

Because of the dynamic nature of the Internet, any web addresses or links contained in this book may have changed since publication and may no longer be valid. The views expressed in this work are solely those of the author and do not necessarily reflect the views of the publisher, and the publisher hereby disclaims any responsibility for them.

Dr. Alicia Holland's Expanding Your Tutoring Business: The Blueprint for Protecting Your Learning Organization

Copyright© 2017 Alicia Holland, EdD. All Rights Reserved.

ISBN-13: 978-1-944346-56-0

Dedication

This book is dedicated to those who are seeking to make a difference in their clients' lives both academically and personally. This profession requires a bold and selfless individual to share his knowledge with the rest of the world while serving as a merchant of hope to individuals who need help with their learning needs.

Georgia, Amaiya, and future children, this book is also dedicated to each of you and to your future success.

Table of Contents

How This Book is Organized ix
Acknowledgments xii
Introduction xiii
My Assumptions xiv

PART I: Protecting Your Tutoring Business Brands 1

    Chapter 1: Understanding Intellectual
                  Property and What to Protect 3

    Chapter 2: Using Types of Agreements in
                  Your Tutoring Practice 9

    Chapter 3: Implementing Systems to
                  Manage Your Intellectual Property 19

**PART II: Data-Driven Strategies for
          Tutoring Business Success** 23

    Chapter 4: Essential Components of
                  Your Tutoring Business Plan 29

    Chapter 5: Federal Laws that Impact
                  Your Tutoring Business 41

    Chapter 6: Reporting Student
                  Progress to Stakeholders 55

PART III: Developing a Quality Control Plan for Your Tutoring Business 59

Chapter 7: Essential Components of a Quality Control Plan 61

Chapter 8: Content Development Process for Your Products 67

Chapter 9: Implementing Quality Assurance Meetings 79

Chapter 10: Creating an Online Project Management System for your Content Team 89

PART IV: Conducting Research in Your Learning Organization 95

Chapter 11: Implementing Focus Groups & Market Research 97

Chapter 12: Disseminating Your Research for Your Learning Organization 107

About the Author.. *112*
References... *114*
Index *113*

How this Book is Organized

Dr. Alicia Holland's *Expanding Your Tutoring Business: The Blue Print for Protecting Your Learning Organization* is is organized into four major parts—the following sections explain what you will find in each part.

Part I: Protecting Your Tutoring Business Brands

In this section, I discuss the diverse types of intellectual property necessary for your tutoring business. Also, you get the chance to take a quick assessment regarding what is considered intellectual property in your own learning organization. When working with tutors and contractors, you also need to protect both yourself and your company. Thus, you will have an opportunity to look at the several types of work agreements, including licensing agreements, and how to keep track of intellectual property licensed or created by your learning organization. It is important to make sure that you implement systems within your learning organization to manage your intellectual property.

Part II: Data-Driven Strategies for Tutoring Business Success

Before we dive into the essential components of a business plan, you will analyze scenarios that are very insightful to your understanding of why business plans are important and why you should have one. In addition, I address the federal laws that will impact your tutoring business and how to create plans that will protect parents, students, and your employees. Last but not least, in this section, you will have an opportunity to create a plan that addresses how you will be reporting student progress to your clients, including stakeholders.

Part III: Developing a Quality Control Plan for Your Tutoring Business

In this part, you will identify the essential components of a quality control plan and learn about the manpower necessary to carry out educational projects that your learning organization may bid on in a proposal solicitation. Also, you will learn what it takes to communicate effectively when dealing with various individuals at different phases of a particular project. You may decide that you want to produce your own content for your clients or target market and will need a process to be successful. Thus, in this section, you will identify the content development process and describe the several types of validity and reliability measures necessary to deem your products as quality, reliable, and valid. Lastly, we cover how to implement quality assurance meetings and create an online project management system for your content team to manage your learning organizational needs.

Part IV: Conducting Research in Your Learning Organization

In this part, I discuss the importance of implementing focus groups and market research into your learning organization to help drive your products and services. You will have a chance to reflect upon some questions that will help you implement and run your own focus groups so that the market research will be effective for your learning organization. Additionally, I will discuss various platforms in which you can disseminate your research for your learning organization.

Where to Go From Here

You have the blueprint to get started, and you should be on the lookout for the next book in the Expanding Your Tutoring Business Book Series. The next step is to join one of Dr. Holland's Mastermind Groups to gain access to exclusive content, network with other tutor business owners, and interact with Dr. Holland so that you can strategically move your tutoring business from good to great.

You can join at www.expandyourtutoringbusinessblog.com

Acknowledgements

I cannot say this enough, but I must give glory to God for helping me realize my potential and purpose in life. Thanks to my editor, Jena Roach, who has helped build confidence in my writing skills and challenged me to expand my ideas.

Introduction

This book is the final part in the series *Expanding Your Tutoring Business* series. It is conceived and created for the independent tutor and courageous educator who desire to take their tutoring business to the next level. My seminal work on tutoring, *Becoming a Better Tutor: A Data-Driven Approach to Tutoring,* has been well received since its first publication in 2010.

This is my first comprehensive book series on tutoring; that is, it serves as the blueprint for individuals to step up their game from a home-based tutoring business to a full-fledged global learning organization that offers tutoring and so much more to clients around the world.

I'm a certified teacher, professional tutor, instructional designer, curriculum developer, online professor, educational consultant, author, and global business owner. I've stepped out on faith to follow my lifelong passion and dream. The information presented in this series is based on insight and actual experiences that I have encountered over the years in building my own global learning organization.

This book series will help you build a solid and successful global learning organization. You'll find advice herein on how to position your learning organization to prosper in such an ever-changing global market. Whether you are a new or veteran tutor, I will show you how to do what you love full-time—helping others learn and grow and sharing your knowledge with the world. My ultimate goal within my professional career and this book series is to inspire and transform others according to their life purpose. But first, you have to believe in yourself and your potential. Now is the time to begin!

My Assumptions

In order to provide you with material to meet your unique situation, I had to make some basic assumptions about your tutoring business. I assume the following:

1. You have intellectual property that you would like to protect for either yourself or your learning organization.
2. You want information on how to protect your intellectual property for your learning organization.
3. You are ready to apply for copyrights, trademarks, or patents for your learning organization.

Part I:
Protecting Your Tutoring Business Brands

CHAPTER 1

Understanding Intellectual Property and What to Protect

Merriam Webster's Online Dictionary (2012) defines intellectual property as:

"Property (as an idea, invention, or process) that derives from the work of the mind or intellect; also: an application, right, or registration relating to this" (1).

Now that you have the definition of intellectual property, you need to identify the various types of intellectual property necessary for your tutoring business. Depending on how your learning organization is structured and the types of products and services offered to clients will depend on what you will need to protect.

Various Types of Intellectual Property Necessary for Your Tutoring Business

While you were planning the beginning of your learning organization, you probably thought of a clever business name with a unique logo that said a lot about your company. Did you know that was your intellectual property and you should protect it? There are three types of intellectual property, which includes the following:

Copyright	Trademark	Patent
The exclusive legal rights to reproduce, publish, sell, or distribute the matter and form of something (as a literary, musical, or artistic work) [Merriam Webster's Online Dictionary, 2012]	A device (as a word) pointing distinctly to the origin or ownership of merchandise to which it is applied and legally reserved to the exclusive use of the owner as maker or seller (Merriam Webster's Online Dictionary, 2012).	Protected by a trademark or a brand name so as to establish proprietary rights analogous to those conveyed by letters patent or a patent(Merriam Webster's Online Dictionary, 2012).

Based upon the above definitions, you can clearly comprehend the importance of intellectual property and why you should protect it. These definitions should help you understand what is needed for your own learning organization.

Copyrights

The first type of intellectual property is copyright. You may already be familiar with copyrights; did you know that you do not necessarily have to copyright your work? Yes, this is true because the work is already protected once you write it down on paper or in an electronic document. However, you cannot impose the copyright in court if the original work has not been properly filed at the United States Copyright Office. This should be done when the work is completed and before it is distributed. If you have a paper book, then you will have to send in hard copies to complete the registration process.

Bottom line, the purpose of copyrighting original work is to protect it from unauthorized individuals. Now that you are creating your own content, you will have both a better understanding of the U.S. Copyright Law and the ability to actually respect it.

Can you identify the types of original work that can be copyrighted for your tutoring business? Well, you have a chance to test your knowledge regarding original works that can be copyrighted by taking the self-assessment below.

Self-Assessment: Can it be copyrighted?			
Directions: Circle Y for Yes and N for No to determine if these works can be copyrighted.			
Books	Y or N	Email Blasts	Y or N
EBooks	Y or N	Lectures	Y or N
Blogs	Y or N	Lessons	Y or N
Workbooks	Y or N	Trainings	Y or N
Website Content	Y or N	Processes	Y or N
Newsletters	Y or N	Tutor Certification Tests	Y or N
Brochures	Y or N	Surveys	Y or N
Sales Copy	Y or N	Agreements	Y or N
Curriculum	Y or N	Business Plans	Y or N
Online Content	Y or N	Online Course Content	Y or N

How did you do? Each of those items can be copyrighted and should be. Now that you have identified the types of Intellectual Property, let's look at the next type of intellectual property that pertains to your learning organization.

Logos and Taglines

This is the second type of Intellectual Property—Logos and Taglines. They are the first impression of your company's image. Therefore, you want to make sure that there is something unique in the logo and tagline that specifically relates to your type of business. They should be special and easy to pronounce in order to resonate with clients. After all, you want your business to be memorable for the right reasons. Protecting your tutoring business' logos and taglines is as easy as applying for a trademark. You can do this one two ways: hiring an intellectual property lawyer or doing it yourself.

Hiring an intellectual property lawyer is a major investment that can be tax deductible, but be prepared to shell out a large retainer just to have access to their "smarts". On the other hand, if you plan on doing it yourself, you need to think about the amount of time that it would take you to research the specific laws regarding your intellectual property. There are many self-help intellectual property resources available from the lawyers themselves, if you choose the latter.

Trade Secrets

The third type of intellectual property is trade secrets. Trade secrets are any information that keeps you in business due to your competitive advantage. Therefore, you will need to keep your processes low key and put in place agreements when hiring additional help for your learning organization. When it comes to trade secrets, you can apply for a patent that focuses on a particular design. Patents can get tricky, so the best advice is to see an intellectual property lawyer and copyright everything. When it comes to intellectual property, it is always best to copyright first. This way, you have protected your intellectual property in the least expensive fashion and it gives you time to gain more knowledge about intellectual property and get a sense of how you want to proceed.

Expert's Advice:

First of all, I suggest visiting an intellectual property lawyer and try to find out what is needed because they can help you with your unique situation. If you are the type that likes to read and research on your own, then you can utilize the resources listed at the back of this book to help you with additional information. Another suggestion is to take a small business course in intellectual property; this would definitely be worth the investment.

If you are coming from the classroom, then keeping your processes to yourself may be challenging. This is mainly because you have been conditioned to share everything with your team, which is great. However, you run a business now. There are some things that must be kept a secret so that you can stay in business. These things relate directly to your intellectual property. Don't ever forget that!

Even when working with the government, you should clearly label proposals in which the information is considered proprietary. This will protect your trade secrets from the public and other competitive bidders who are looking to see how they performed in response to your proposal.

In my personal opinion, companies should be allowed to describe their services and make general references when placing bids for government work. As I have previously said, copyright everything because there are intellectual property thieves lurking around to snag the next big idea. You can also check the U.S. Copyright website to search for documents that have been copyrighted and to make sure that your work is properly displayed. You will receive copyright certificates in the regular mail about three to four months after you have applied for your copyright for a specific work(s).

CHAPTER 2

Using Types of Agreements in Your Tutoring Practice

When it was just you, it really didn't matter about being organized. Now that you're a company with employees, it's crucial for your business's success. Depending on how you run your learning organization, you will need only a few of the agreements. Let's get to the legal aspect of dealing with contractors. In order to protect your company, you need to be aware of the types of work agreements necessary to do business.

There are four types of agreements that will be needed to ensure that you are doing good business and protecting yourself.

- Work-for-Hire Agreements
- Tutor Agreements
- Non-Compete Agreements
- Project Agreements
- Confidentiality Agreements

1. Work-for-Hire Agreements

These should be given to all contractors in which you desire to work with for your projects. They are key components to constructing a work for hire. You can typically find templates in Microsoft Word, a lawyer software such as My Attorney Home and Business, or on the Internet.

When constructing a work-for-hire agreement, you should ensure that the copyright holder and project scope are clearly identified. Make sure the original signatures are obtained.

2. Tutor Agreements

The second agreement, Tutor Agreement, should be given to all tutors. You will quickly discover that tutors will leave for various reasons, and you do not want to find yourself without clients or in a legal battle with former tutors. There are a few points that should be clearly outlined in the tutoring agreement to protect your business interests. To help develop these key points, answer the following questions to assist you in crafting your tutor agreement.

1. What is the purpose of this tutor agreement?

   _____
   _____
   _____
   _____
   _____
   _____

2. How will tutors be compensated? In other words, what services will tutors get paid for?

   _____
   _____
   _____
   _____
   _____

3. Will tutors get paid for time outside of their tutoring sessions? Why or why not?

_____
_____
_____
_____
_____
_____

4. What is your non-compete policy or clause?

_____
_____
_____
_____
_____
_____

5. What are the specific restrictions regarding the tutor position?

_____
_____
_____
_____
_____
_____

6. How will you communicate the confidentiality and non-disclosure agreement?

_____
_____
_____
_____
_____
_____

7. How will tutors return this agreement? Will they fax, scan and email, or snail mail it?

_____
_____
_____
_____
_____

These questions will help you focus on the key points that are necessary when doing business with tutors.

Expert's Advice:

When you are creating these agreements for tutors, you will quickly begin to see some similarities and start questioning whether you need all those agreements. The answer is—YES! You may find that you can condense some forms, but the key is to ensure that tutors are very clear about what they are signing so that everyone understands what is expected of them.

The bottom line is to always protect both yourself and your learning organization because you never know when it comes to hiring tutors. Tutors will come and go, which makes your agreements very important.

3. Non-Compete Agreements

The third agreement can be implemented into the tutor agreement or you can choose to have a separate agreement regarding any non-compete agreements. You can also have a paragraph included in the tutor agreement. Whatever you decide, it should be clearly labeled. Keep in mind, the purpose of a non-compete agreement is to ensure that your tutors won't steal your clients.

Answer the following questions to help you create your non-compete clause.

1. How long will this non-compete agreement be effective?

2. Will this non-compete agreement be under certain conditions? If so, what are those conditions?

3. What are the consequences for breaching the agreement?

4. How will you define competition? Will this also include soliciting, communicating, and using unauthorized use of proprietary materials? Why or why not?

5. How will you communicate the company's rights regarding this non-compete agreement to tutors?

_____
_____
_____
_____
_____

6. Will you have tutors initial this paragraph of the tutor agreement, in addition to, providing a full signature at the end of the agreement? Why or why not?

_____
_____
_____
_____
_____

These six questions will definitely help you brainstorm the information that should be included in the non-compete clause.

4. Project Agreements

The fourth agreement regards additional projects such as curriculum development. Also, project agreements should be used when hiring freelance contractors to work on special projects such as writing, web design, or graphic design projects. When crafting the project agreement, you need to include key information. Here are some questions that can help you identify the vital material for project agreements.

1. Who is the agreement between?
   _____
   _____
   _____
   _____
   _____

2. How will you assign a specific reference number or code to projects?
   _____
   _____
   _____
   _____
   _____

3. When will the project begin and end? What are the terms?
   _____
   _____
   _____
   _____
   _____

4. What are the deliverables?
   _____
   _____
   _____
   _____
   _____

5. Where do you submit these deliverables?
   _____
   _____
   _____
   _____
   _____

6. What is the flat fee pay?
   _____
   _____
   _____
   _____
   _____

7. Who owns the final product? How many pages or lessons can the contractor use for the portfolio of their choice?
   _____
   _____
   _____
   _____
   _____

8. How can this project be terminated?
   _____
   _____
   _____
   _____
   _____

9. What is the dispute resolution policy?

_____
_____
_____
_____
_____
_____

Expert's Advice:

Regardless of the services that are provided, each contractor should be given each of the forms except the tutor agreement unless they desire to tutor as well.

5. Confidentiality and Non-Disclosure Agreements

These should also be included in non-disclosure agreements. When crafting confidentiality and non-disclosure agreements, there are some key things that should be addressed, such as determining what the contract is all about. Keep in mind, the purpose of confidentiality and non-disclosure agreements are to protect your trade secrets that make your tutoring company competitive.

Below are specific points that must be addressed to avoid misunderstandings:

- Identify the purpose
- State who develops the products, trade secrets, proprietary rights
- Include a statement explaining that each contractor must agree to keep information confidential, not disclosing any information without the company's written approval
- Mention owner of the copyright
- Include original signature and date when the agreement goes into effect

The confidentiality agreement will have some similar verbiage as the tutor agreement, but the key difference is that this agreement will cover other projects and tasks beyond tutoring, such as curriculum development.

CHAPTER 3

Implementing Systems to Manage Your Intellectual Property

When it comes to your intellectual property, you need to be organized because you may forget what you have already created. Most importantly, you want to be able to identify themes that may help you develop more intellectual property to grow your tutoring practice. There are several ways that you could develop a system to maintain records of your intellectual property activity, including the following:

Use Folders	Safety Deposit Box	Security Box
Secured Cabinet	Keep it On Hand	Electronic Storage

Each of these methods works when trying to maintain records. Whatever method is used, individuals should always keep an extra copy on hand, just in case, it is needed or hard drives malfunction. There are some online file storage websites that allows you to access files anywhere and is definitely an investment.

Describing What It Means to License a Product

Do you have products that could be licensed? Are you wondering how to license a product to another individual or company? In this chapter, you will learn what it takes to license your products.

Licensing a product simply means to give individuals or companies the right to reproduce or deliver content for a certain amount of time. This type of process can get tricky, if an agreement is not in place. Let's look at a few scenarios regarding licensing products to other businesses or individuals.

Scenario 1: "Giveth and Taketh"

Travis, an online learning organization owner, offered a continuing education program for teachers. He offered some unique courses directly related to teaching mathematics. One of the math professions organizations contacted Travis to inquire about purchasing a license to deliver one of the courses for their own math program. Since he copyrighted the content, he could license out the material. Travis's agreement consisted of a verbal agreement, and he transferred the rights to them. A year later, the math professional organization added two of the same courses without paying an annual license fee to Travis because they owned the copyright.

What could have been done differently? Do you think that Travis could have gotten a better deal for his learning organization? Why or why not?

Expert's Advice:

First of all, Travis should have drawn up a license agreement that included specific information for both parties. Here are some guidelines to help create a licensing agreement. They are the following:

1. **Identify the Parties in the Agreement:** You should include full legal name of both parties or legal business name and the business address. This will enable anyone to quickly determine those involved in the agreement.

2. **Set Terms for Licensing Agreement:** It is very important to set a specific term for licensing the content so that there will not be any confusion.

3. **Determine a Licensing Fee:** Licensing fees are recurring based on the terms of the licensing agreement. For example, individuals or companies can determine an annual fee that can be charged to keep revenue coming in.

4. **Clearly State that You Hold the Copyright:** You want to make sure that you communicate who holds the copyright so there are not any surprises.

5. **Sign and Date the Agreement:** The agreement is not official until both parties have signed an original signature and dated the agreement.

6. **Notarize the Agreement:** This is a very important type of agreement so it would be a great idea to notarize the agreement to ensure that the document is original and official.

If you are uncertain about something in the agreement, you could always hire an intellectual property lawyer, if your budget permits. Nevertheless, these are some guidelines that you should consider when creating license agreements.

Part II:
Data-Driven Strategies for Tutoring Business Success

> "Vision always deals with the future. Indeed, vision is where tomorrow begins, for it expresses what you and others who share the vision will be working hard to create" (Nanus, 1992, p.8).

You may have heard that you need a business plan to start a business and, to some extent, this is true. Depending on how you entered the tutoring industry, it will determine how elaborate your tutoring business plan should be. A business plan is needed to get funding for your company, and it is a great strategy to have as a business owner. Below are several scenarios to get an idea of how business plans can impact your tutoring business.

Let's look at a tutor who started out as a home-based business owner.

Scenario 1: "Ready or Not…Here I come"

Bobbi, an English Language Arts (ELA) tutor, who specialized in helping students with learning disabilities, started a home-based tutoring business during the summer. She decided that she would enlist three additional clients to keep her schedule full during the fall term since she was still teaching in the classroom full-time. After three years of building her clientele, she was able to move her home-based tutoring practice to an actual office. At that point, Bobbi consulted with a business advisor and quickly learned that she needed a business plan to expand because she wanted to apply for a small business loan with a microlender. Before she could do that, she needed to establish a new company that was a Limited Liability Company (LLC). Rather than provide misinformation, the business advisor referred her to a tax advisor of her choice. Bobbi ended up hiring a consultant to complete her business plan, but she never did anything with it because her business was not ready for the growth which Bobbi anticipated.

If you were in Bobbi's situation, what would you have done? Do you think that the business plan was necessary at this point? Why or why not?

Expert's Advice:

Bobbi did all of the right things before expanding her tutoring practice. The reality is a business plan needs to be in place, just to see how things work. However, the most important thing is vision.

Once you have your business plan in place, you will better understand what I mean. Personally, I used my business plan as a roadmap, and it did come in handy at a later time. Keep in mind, this was several years after working as a home-based tutor. My number one goal was, and still is, my vision. This helped me focused on building my clientele and providing quality tutoring services. If you are at this point, I would recommend that you do the same.

Let's look at a different situation regarding business plans.

Scenario 2: "I will do It Myself"

Roman, an online math tutor, decided that he wanted to take his physical tutoring practice online. At first, this was very scary because his current clients were skeptical of being tutored online. Luckily, the clients tried it out and were very pleased with the results. He later discovered that he needed additional tutors to help out, which meant he needed more money for developing a curriculum and so forth. Roman had created a business plan and often referred to it. He was pleased to learn that his business was in sync with his business goals. Given that his tutoring business was online, Roman was able to self-fund his newly found expenses. The good news was Roman loaned the company the money, which gave him incredible tax breaks and owner's equity into the business.

How do you feel about Roman self-funding his own tutoring company? Would you be willing to do the same thing? Why or why not?

Expert's Advice:

Roman was very blessed in this situation. I guess he read my first book, *Becoming a Better Tutor: A Data-Driven Approach to Tutoring*. If you are able to self-fund your company without any business loans, you are doing very well. Keep in mind that, at some point, after you have expanded and are ready to work with the government or other major organizations, you will need to take out a business loan. Hopefully, you will be financially ready on both a personal and business level.

The bottom line is that you will need to start applying for business credit, but truly, this will depend on your tutoring business needs. All of these goals can be identified in your business plan, but it may not materialize until a later date. In other words, don't get frustrated. Timing is everything, and you will get your chance to shine—that is, your plans to expand will manifest.

Scenario 3: "Preparation is King"

Corey, a math and reading tutor, decided that he wanted to apply for tutoring with school districts under the No Child Left Behind (NCLB) Act. After looking at the application, he realized that it requires program information and financials for his tutoring company. Specifically, the state asked for the following: (a) budgets; (b) program costs; (c) business plan; and (d) Certified Public Account (CPA) financial statements.

Corey was a little bit nervous, but his accountant helped him understand what was required of him. Corey outsourced the program portion of the application to a respected, educational consultant, while he and his accountant worked on the fiscal accountability. Corey was very thankful for keeping up with his business plan so he was able to submit it. After 6-8 weeks of waiting, Corey received a letter in the mail that was from the state's Department of Education. To his surprise, Corey's learning organization was approved as a Supplemental Educational Services (SES) tutor provider for that specific state.

If you were in Corey's situation, how would your business plan measure up to what the state was looking for in SES Tutor Providers?

Expert's Advice:

Corey was able to reap the benefits of a business plan in this situation. This is a great example of how Corey updated his business plan according to his learning organization's needs, and it paid off. Therefore, the best advice that I can provide is to have a business plan to see how you are doing because there are a variety of opportunities and challenges that will present itself. When they do, you will need to review your business plan to see if this is in the direction in which you need to go. For your tutoring practice, I will share with you the components that are essential to see your business expand.

CHAPTER 4

Essential Components of a Business Plan

The essential components of a business plan should include at least eight categories of your learning organization. These eight categories include the following:

While I cannot tell you what to put in your business plan because I do not know the specifics about your tutoring business, I can definitely guide you in the process.

Here are some questions to help you build your own business plan:

Products and Services

1. How would you introduce your learning organization to potential investors?

   _____
   _____
   _____
   _____
   _____

2. How would you describe your products and services?

   _____
   _____
   _____
   _____
   _____

3. How are your products and services different from your competitors?

   _____
   _____
   _____
   _____
   _____

Here's a summary of the questions to help you understand how to answer each question pertaining to this category:

Question	Purpose of Question
CATEGORY: PRODUCTS AND SERVICES	
1	Pertains to the introduction or overview of your tutoring company. When answering this question, you should include the following information: (a) business name and location; (b) legal structure; (c) principle owners; (d) summary of business; (e) history of the business; and (f) purpose of the business. Each piece of information will definitely give prospective investors an idea of what your business is about. A Strengths, Weaknesses, Opportunities, Threats (**SWOT**) Analysis should also be included so that you can point out both strengths and challenges that may currently exist or may occur in the near future.
2	Dedicated to your products and services. This is your chance to go in detail regarding the types of tutoring in which you conduct and so forth. If you have additional products such as books and workbooks for students, then this information would go here too.
3	Provides you the opportunity to set yourself apart from your competition. This will also give you a chance to see how your tutoring business measures up to the competition.

Office Operations Plan

1. How would you describe your business location?
   _____
   _____
   _____
   _____
   _____
   _____

2. How would you describe your office space?

   _____
   _____
   _____
   _____
   _____

3. Do you have an office floor plan available? Why or why not?

   _____
   _____
   _____
   _____
   _____

4. How would you describe your tutoring inventory? Is it physical or virtual? Why or why not?

   _____
   _____
   _____
   _____
   _____

5. What skills and experiences are necessary to run the office?

   _____
   _____
   _____
   _____
   _____

Here's a summary of the questions to help you understand how to answer each question pertaining to this category:

CATEGORY: OFFICE OPERATIONS PLAN	
Question	Purpose of Question
1	Pertains to describing the business location. In other words, you should provide detail on why you selected the office space. You should also include business hours as well.
2	Provides the opportunity to discuss your office space, along with identifying the parking area for customers.
3	Focuses on the office floor plan. Typically, the floor plan helps to support Question 2.
4	Affords tutor business owners the opportunity to reflect on their tutoring inventory. Depending on whether individuals are managing a physical or virtual tutoring company, it will determine how inventory is stored. Of course, office supplies inventory will be included as well.
5	Addresses the management plan. This is where you would describe the type of skills and experiences necessary to run the office from day to day. You may find that you could do it, but quickly discover that it would be best to pay a qualified individual. This will free up time for you to focus solely on business strategy.

Market Analysis

1. What are the industry trends?

   _____
   _____
   _____
   _____
   _____

2. How would you describe the market?

   _____
   _____
   _____
   _____
   _____

3. What is the size of your target market?

   _____
   _____
   _____
   _____
   _____

4. How would you document demand for your market and services?

   _____
   _____
   _____
   _____
   _____

5. What is your analysis of the competition in the tutoring industry?

   _____
   _____
   _____
   _____
   _____

6. How can your tutoring business find a niche in the market to fill the void?

_____
_____
_____
_____
_____

Here's a summary of the questions to help you understand how to answer each question pertaining to this category:

\multicolumn{2}{c}{CATEGORY: MARKET ANALYSIS}	
Question	Purpose of Question
1	Allows you to focus on the trends that are emerging or future trends for the industry.
2	Focuses on the market in both a general and specific nature.
3	In order to answer this question, Question 2 must be answered. This gives individuals the opportunity to zone in on niche markets.
4	Challenges you to obtain letter of recommendations, references, and client testimonials. It's one thing to be good, but how will you convince others that they need your services and products?
5	After searching the market, what did you find out and how does it relate to your competition. This is what you should focus on when answering this question.
6	Addresses you finding the "missing key" in the industry. In other words, where does your business fit in a soon-to-be saturated market and how to keep it there?

Sales Strategy

1. What is your pricing policy?

2. How do you intend to reach your target market?

3. How does your competition reach their target market?

4. How will the product be made available and where can customers purchase it?

Here's a summary of the questions to help you understand how to answer them:

	CATEGORY: SALES STRATEGY
Question	Purpose of Question
1	Pertains to how you will justify your pricing for both services and products. This will also be the perfect time to start looking at introducing tutoring packages rather than hourly rates. You want to provide your clients with value. As you already know, clients will need more than one tutoring session.
2	Challenges you to create a marketing plan so that you can reach your target market. In other words, you need to find out where your target market hangs out and let them know about both your products and services.
3	Focuses on finding out what your competition is doing and keeping track of it. You need to know how your competition reaches their target market.
4	Encourages you to plan out how your products will be made available and what forms of payment in which your company will accept. This is very important if you plan on selling products such as eBooks, workbooks, merchandise, and other accessories.

Management Plan

1. How would you describe your business background?

_____
_____
_____
_____
_____

2. What is the management experience?

   _____
   _____
   _____
   _____
   _____

3. What is the academic background of key employees/contractors within your tutoring business?

   _____
   _____
   _____
   _____
   _____

4. What are the job descriptions of key employees/contractors?

   _____
   _____
   _____
   _____
   _____

5. How are employees and contractors compensated?

   _____
   _____
   _____
   _____
   _____

Here's a summary of the questions to help you understand how to answer each question pertaining to this category:

CATEGORY: MANAGEMENT PLAN	
Question	Purpose of Question
1	Focuses on how the business got started. You can dive in to how it relates to both the mission and vision statement.
2	Addresses the management experience. It would be a great idea to list your managerial and leadership skills from other jobs and clearly explaining how it relates to the tutoring business in its current form.
3	Fixates on highlighting the educational background and experiences. This is very important if you plan on working with major learning organizations because they will need to see it and will call references to ensure the quality of your services and products.
4	Challenges you to plan, in advance, the various job descriptions of key positions, including contractor positions. If you do this now, it will be easier on you. In the first book of this series, it provides support to do this task.
5	Provides an opportunity to create a pay structure for both employees and contractors. This piece of information, along with other valuable knowledge can be found in book two of this series.

Financial Analysis

1. What are anticipated start-up costs for your tutoring business or expansion?

_____
_____
_____
_____
_____
_____

2. How will you verify income statements, balance sheets, income tax returns, and personal finances?

_____
_____
_____
_____
_____

Here's a summary of the questions to help you understand how to answer each question pertaining to this category:

Question	Purpose of Question
\multicolumn{2}{c}{CATEGORY: FINANCIAL ANALYSIS}
1	Focuses on start-up costs. You may already have some of your resources, but you will still incur expenses and should document them appropriately.
2	Encourages you to figure out how to gather the financial statements necessary to get an accurate picture of the business. If you haven't already, you need to invest in both an accountant and some type of accounting software such as QuickBooks or Peachtree.

Supporting Documents

Whatever you think that will show your business in the best light is what you include here.

These questions will help you get started with building a tailor-made business plan for your learning organization.

CHAPTER 5

Federal Laws that Impact Your Tutoring Business

As with any other industry, you have to be aware of laws that may threaten your business. In education, there are federal laws that can impact the way in which your tutoring business operates, especially if you are working with the federal government to provide tutoring services to low-income students. Whatever the case may be, you should still design your tutoring business to adhere to these laws so that it can be considered a quality and reputable learning organization.

Whether you decide to work with the federal government or not, you should still understand and be cognizant of the federal laws that impact your tutoring business. This will keep you in federal—compliance and bring you multiple opportunities to expand your tutoring business because of the high standards that are set for your learning organization. There are six federal laws that will impact your tutoring business, which include the following:

Let's look at the laws that impact the learners in which you serve.

Elementary and Secondary Education Act (ESEA)

The ESEA is the major federal statute that was passed in 1965. According to the U.S. Department of Education (2011), "President Lyndon Johnson signed the ESEA into law on April 1965 (p. 1). Basically, this law granted equal access to public education for all children. In 2002, President George W. Bush signs the No Child Left Behind (NCLB) Act into Law (U.S. Dept. Ed, 2011, p. 1). The bi-partisan NCLB Act was a major milestone for the twenty-first century because it challenged states to set education standards and increase school accountability.

According to the U.S. Department of Education (2011), "The ESEA reauthorization usually occurs every five years; however, NCLB has governed elementary and secondary education for nearly a decade, and congress has yet to act to fix some of the law's flaws" (p. 2).

Expert's Advice:

This law impacts your tutoring business because it deals with education. You need to have a sense to where you are going. If you happen to run a SES program, there's a possibility that your program can be cancelled due to the new ESEA flexibility waivers. Don't fret though, there are other opportunities available to provide educational services.

Family Educational Rights and Privacy Act (FERPA) Laws

If you are a private learning organization, which most tutors are, it is still a great idea to comply to this law. On the other hand, learning organizations that are being federally funded will have to comply to this law. Students who are under 18 will have parents exercise their rights on behalf of their children. However, once students turn 18, they can exercise their own rights. The FERPA Act allows the following:

- The Right to Access to Education Records
- The Right to Amendment of Education Records
- The Right to Control over Disclosure of Personally Identifiable Information
- The Right to File a Complaint with the Department (U.S. Dept. Education, 2011, p. 1).

Now, let's look at the remaining laws that impact any employee or contractor, hired to work at your learning organization.

Equal Employment Opportunity (EEO)

The EEO has a lot of bases that individuals are covered under by the federal law. These bases are the following:

- Race, Color, Religion, Sex, National Origin
- Disability
- Age
- Sex (Wages)
- Genetics
- Retaliation (EEOC.gov, 2012, n.p.)

You should always hire individuals based upon their performance during the hiring process for your learning organization. To ensure that all federal employment laws are followed, it is a great idea to create job descriptions. That way, potential applicants will know that they are being hired based upon their knowledge and skills pertaining to the job description.

Age Discrimination in Employment Act (ADEA) of 1967

Age Discrimination in Employment Act (ADEA) of 1967 protects applicants and employees 40 years of age or older from discrimination based on age in hiring, promotion, discharge, pay, fringe benefits, job training, classification, referral, and other aspects of employment (EEOC.gov, 2012). When hiring tutors, age should not be a factor. Therefore, it is very important to have a hiring process in place that does not break any of the federal laws and are deemed ethical hiring practices.

Civil Rights Act of 1964

The Civil Rights Act of 1964 "protects applicants and employees from discrimination in hiring, promotion, discharge, pay, fringe benefits, job training, classification, referral, and other aspects of employment, on the basis of race, color, religion, sex (including pregnancy), or national origin" (EEOC.gov, 2012). Just like the Age Discrimination in Employment Act of 1967, the Civil Rights Act of 1964 can also be addressed by designing a quality hiring process that focus on talent acquisition and your company's core values and mission statement.

Americans with Disabilities Act of 1990

The Americans with Disabilities Act of 1990 makes it "illegal to discriminate against a qualified person with a disability in the private sector and in state and local governments" (EEOC.gov, 2012). It is very important that you set up your office space to cater to clients or employees who may have special needs and need accommodations to be successful in either their tutoring session or job assignment. Also, you should look for office space that has an ADA-Accessible Bathroom to utilized while at your office.

Rights Protection Plans and Student Health and Safety Plan

At this point, you should be thinking about how you will address these two federal laws that pertain to students and their families. There are two types of plans that your tutoring business will need, which are the following (a) Students' Rights Protection Plan; and (b) Student Health and Safety Plan.

Students' Rights Protection Plan

A Rights Protection Plan caters to protecting both students and employees regarding their federal, state, and local civil rights protections. On the other hand, a Student Health and Safety Plan will address specific health and safety issues regarding tutoring services. Examples include protecting confidentiality, consistent tutor scheduling, background checks, and so forth.

Below are some questions to help you develop your own students' rights protection plan. They are the following:

1. How do you document tutoring sessions?

   _____
   _____
   _____
   _____
   _____

2. How will progress reports be delivered?

   _____
   _____
   _____
   _____
   _____

3. How do you protect confidential information such as incoming faxes or client files?

4. Do you have a written third-party authorization form on file for clients? Why or why not?

5. When communicating with tutors, how do you protect the student's name?

6. Do you have some type of reference code when referring to clients? Why or why not?

7. How do you verify contact information such as mailing addresses, phone numbers, and email addresses?

8. Do you send test emails to verify correct information? Why or why not?

9. How do you handle mail communication? Do you send it as certified mail? Why or why not?

10. When hiring employees, including contractors, do you have them sign a non-disclosure agreement? Why or why not?

These are ten questions to help with developing your students' rights protection plan.

Employees' Rights Protection Plan

When it comes to developing this plan, individuals need to create a hiring system that supports each of these acts. In Dr. Holland-Johnson's EYBT: The Blue Print for Hiring Tutors and Contractors for Your Learning Organization, there are guidelines and strategies to help you develop your program. If you hire a Human Resources (HR) company such as the Automatic Data Processing (ADP) Company, they will help you so that you can be in compliance with these federal laws as well.

Expert's Advice:

Each of these questions will help you identify safeguards for your tutoring business. Some common types of safeguards include the following:

a. Documented tutoring sessions
b. Electronic fax
c. Third-party authorization forms
d. Coded communication with tutors
e. Test emails
f. Secured envelope
g. Non-disclosure agreement
h. Hiring process

Each of these safeguards protects your tutoring business, clients, and employees. Therefore, it is in your best interest to implement a variety of safeguards.

Student Health and Safety Plan

Have you considered a plan to protect students' health and safety? In tutoring, you may also wonder what type of health and safety issues may arise. There are six different areas in which tutors can protect their business and their clients.

These six areas include the following:

Tutoring Service Delivery	Consistent Tutor Scheduled	Focused, Learning Environment
Confidentiality	Emergency Procedures	Background Checks and Fingerprinting

Depending on whether your tutoring business is online or face-to-face will effect how these six areas are addressed. In an effort to assist you with creating your own student health and safety plan, here are some questions to help guide you:

1. How are you delivering tutoring services? (Face-to-Face, online, etc.)

   _____
   _____
   _____
   _____
   _____

2. How do you communicate to parents how tutoring services are delivered?

   _____
   _____
   _____
   _____
   _____

3. How do you protect your student's information?

_____
_____
_____
_____
_____

4. How do you communicate your confidentiality statement to your clients?

_____
_____
_____
_____
_____

5. What emergency procedures do you have in place regarding your tutoring services?

_____
_____
_____
_____
_____

6. How do you communicate your emergency procedures to your clients?

_____
_____
_____
_____
_____

7. How do you screen tutors prior to scheduling them for tutoring assignments?

8. What process is in place to communicate to clients how tutors are qualified to teach in your learning organization?

9. Do you assign the same tutor for an entire tutoring assignment per learner? Why or why not?

10. How do you communicate tutoring assignments to both clients and tutors?

11. How would you describe a typical tutoring session to your clients?

_____
_____
_____
_____
_____

12. Do you have a policy in place regarding asking any personal questions or information? Why or why not?

_____
_____
_____
_____
_____

13. How do you document tutoring sessions? Are they recorded? Why or why not?

_____
_____
_____
_____
_____

14. How is this communicated to your clients and tutors?

_____
_____
_____
_____
_____

Each of these questions will help you create your very own plan to address students' health and safety concerns.

> **Expert's Advice:**
>
> It is very important to have a student health and safety plan to prevent any legal litigation. Also, this shows that you are a professional who is providing quality tutoring services in a safe learning environment. Most importantly, if you plan on working with the federal government by providing SES tutoring services to low-income families, then you will definitely need these services. Just look at it this way, you will be ahead of yourself when it comes time to expanding into the government sector.

CHAPTER

Reporting Student Progress to Stakeholders

How often do you report student progress? This is a question that most tutors ask when starting out with their tutoring business. Even after starting their business, the frequency of reporting student progress changes.

There are a variety of ways to collect data and you should be collecting a variety to truly document significant student progress. Before we go in detail, let's reflect upon what you are already doing so that you can appreciate your efforts and have room for inspiration.

Self-Reflection

Please answer these two questions:

1. How do you document student progress?
_____
_____
_____
_____

2. How often do you report student progress?

_____
_____
_____
_____

For now, use these great questions to reflect on your tutoring practice.

Let's look at the types of data that can be collected regarding student progress. Below you will find both the types of data and their purposes to help students:

TYPES OF DATA COLLECTED IN TUTORING SESSIONS		
Mode of Data Collection	Method Collected	Purpose of Data Collected
Monitoring Notes	Qualitative	Monitoring notes should be taken during the tutoring session. While learners are solving a problem or completing a short mini-assessment, this time should be dedicated to making notes regarding the learner's progress. These notes are qualitative in nature because tutors are collecting data that can only be achieved in a tutoring session. For example, tutors are expected to record the following: (a) learner's progress; (b) learning objectives; (c) attitude/effort; (d) and focus on the next steps for the learner.
Instructional Learning Plan	Qualitative and Quantitative	The instructional plan should be constructed directly after the pre and post assessments and tutoring consultation. The instructional plan shows the learning objectives that need to be covered in tutoring and assessment results to ensure that students are progressing according to the plan. If any changes are needed, then the changes can be communicated on the monthly progress report.

TYPES OF DATA COLLECTED IN TUTORING SESSIONS		
Mode of Data Collection	Method Collected	Purpose of Data Collected
Progress Reports	Qualitative and Quantitative	Progress reports share information gleaned from both monitoring notes and assessments such as mini-assessments and progress monitoring assessments. These types of reports should be at least 1-2 pages and written in a format that clients can easily read. It is recommended to send these updates out monthly by the first week of each month. This can be done either electronically or via regular mail.
Pre and Post Assessments	Quantitative	Pre and post assessments should be given before and after a tutoring program. These assessments will show student growth and most importantly, it will show how effective the learner's tutoring program and its impact on student achievement. These assessments should be both validated and reliable to be considered a quality assessment of student's skills.
Progress Monitoring Assessments	Quantitative	Progress monitoring assessments are used to measure student achievement throughout their tutoring program. These assessments are typically designed to end in one-hour tutoring session and range from 15-25 questions. These results should be communicated immediately to clients and can be included on the monthly progress report.
Mini-Assessment	Qualitative and Quantitative	Mini-assessments are used to measure student achievement during a tutoring program. These assessments are typically designed to finish within 10-15 minutes at the very end of the tutoring session. Each mini-assessment range from 5-10 questions or one essay item with several parts. These results should be included in the monitoring notes and on the monthly progress report.

Expert's Advice:

Each of these types of data shows how students are progressing and the data is triangulated. In other words, the data shows student progress from both a qualitative and quantitative measure. This is how you provide data-driven tutoring and stay in demand because your clients will see significant growth if they attend their tutoring sessions regularly, follow your advice and the student learning plan, and do their part as a learner. If you are working with minor clients, the same applies, but parents are expected to do their part as well. That way, tutoring will be effective and rewarding to all parties involved.

In this chapter, you had an opportunity to create your own students' rights protection plan and student health and safety plan. Now, it's time to work on a quality control plan for your learning organization.

Part III:
Developing a Quality Control Plan for Your Tutoring Business

Content Development Process for Your Products

How do you ensure that your business is providing quality products and services? You need to have a process in mind that will focus on keeping your reputation as a tutor soaring. The only way to do that is to have some type of plan to address quality control matters. Your clients are paying for your work and your ultimate goal is to ensure that you provide quality tutoring services. Therefore, the importance of a quality control plan can either make or break your tutoring business.

CHAPTER 7

Essential Components of a Quality Control Plan

What is a quality control plan? A quality control plan helps businesses ensure that their products and services adhere to a specific requirement that produces quality results and products. There are certain components necessary to create an effective quality control plan. These components include the following:

Essential Components of a Quality Control Plan
1. Purpose
2. Project Quality Control Requirements
3. Organizational Chart showing Responsibilities
4. Communications Plan
5. Format and Schedule for Checking Product Deliverables
6. Format and Schedule for Documenting all comments, issues, and responses

Let's look at each component and see how it applies to your tutoring business needs. Before you can adequately complete a quality control plan, you must answer some questions. They are listed below:

1. What is the purpose of a quality control plan for your learning organization?

   _____
   _____
   _____
   _____
   _____
   _____

2. What type of projects will your learning organization participate now and in the future?

   _____
   _____
   _____
   _____
   _____
   _____

3. How does your current organizational chart support current and future projects?

   _____
   _____
   _____
   _____
   _____
   _____

4. What is your plan for communicating with your independent contractors assigned to the project?

5. What is your current review process for products?

6. How will you communicate this review process to contractors? Will it include a schedule? Why or why not?

7. How will you document all concerns regarding the project? Will you keep a paper trail? Why or why not?

> ### Expert's Advice:
>
> A quality control plan is needed for your tutoring business. Once you continue to expand, you may want to start selling some of your curriculum products. Therefore, buyers will want to know how the products are deemed reliable and valid. You have what you need to get started with your own quality control plan. You will find that it is tailored to your learning organization and should not be shared with others. This is considered your learning organization's intellectual property.

Organizational Chart for Managing Educational Projects in your Tutoring Business

Whether you are designing lessons or assessment items, your tutoring business will need to have some type of noticeable plan to oversee projects. Below is a typical organizational chart that caters to projects involving lessons and assessment items:

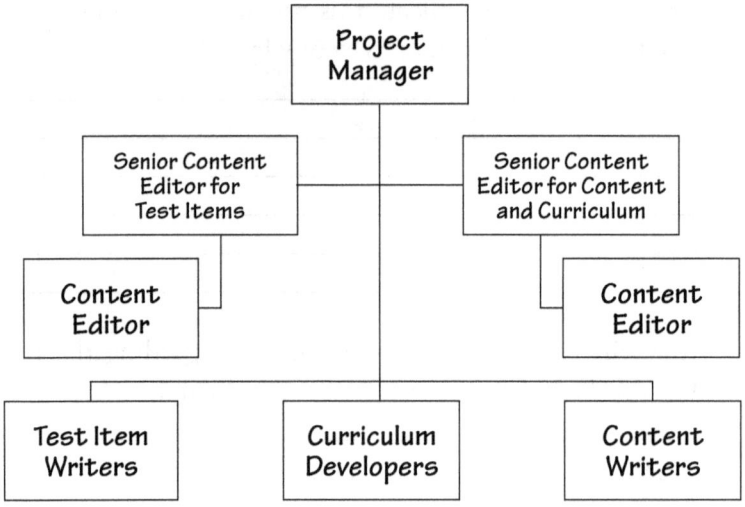

This organizational chart shows what can be done with educational projects. If there happens to be more than one content area, then you want to include that on your chart.

Let's look at the purpose of each role:

Role	Purpose
Project Manager	Responsible for scheduling project update meetings, completing reports, and delivery confirmations.
Senior Content Editor	Responsible for reviewing content submitted for review. Provide feedback regarding first draft of content and working closely with the content editor.
Content Editor	Responsible for content editing and line editing to elevate the quality of the writing.
Item Writers	Responsible for writing test items according to the learning organization's specifications.
Curriculum Developers	Responsible for developing curriculum according to the learning organization's specifications.
Content Writers	Responsible for writing content according to the learning organization's specifications.

Here are some questions that will help you better analyze your situation when curriculum development arises. They are the following:

1. How much funding can you allocate to each position?

2. How often will you start projects throughout the year?

3. Will you have curriculum developers on-call? Why or why not?

_____
_____
_____
_____
_____

4. How will you communicate project deadlines?

_____
_____
_____
_____
_____

5. Will you allow flexible deadlines? Why or why not?

_____
_____
_____
_____
_____

Please keep in mind that contractors are very persistent about following up with you. Therefore, you need to know what you want and communicate that to them. The reality is you are a buyer of their services so they have to wait for your decision. The same is true for them as well. In a nutshell, it works both ways.

CHAPTER 8

Content Development Process for Your Products

We talked about a review process earlier in the chapter, but it pertained to you reviewing your contractor's work for a specific project. In this section, the focus is on the review process for your learning organization's services and products. As you begin to expand, you will quickly discover that there are many types of products that can be offered that will compliment your current offerings.

Below you will find a review process that can be used for products such as workbooks, eBooks, books, and other products of your choice.

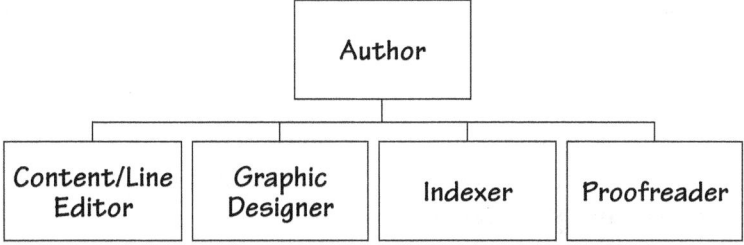

This is the basic content development process for any content-related products. Different individuals should perform each of these roles, especially the editing, indexing, and proofreading. If you are the author of the materials, you will quickly realize that you do not have that kind of time. Therefore, it is just better to stay focused on the content and direction of the creative work.

Let's look at each type of role, its purpose, and a typical budget to expect when it comes time to plan those types of projects.

Role	Purpose	Typical Budget
Author	Creates or develops content for the learning organization.	$500 to $5,000. Depends on content and word count.
Graphic Designer	Designs book covers, book jackets, and other graphic design services.	$100 to $500. Depends on content and word count.
Content Editor	Edits content and is responsible for ensuring content is elevated.	$100 to $1,000. Depends on content and word count.
Line Editor	Edits content line-by-line for ways to elevate the content.	$100 to $1,000. Depends on content and word count.
Indexer	Creates an index at the back of the book for a professional touch.	$100 to $1,000. Depends on content and word count.
Proofreader	Provides the final read for a written work.	$100 to $500. Depends on content and word count.

Each of the roles is very important and it may be a good idea to build a working relationship with such contractors.

> **Expert's Advice:**
>
> You may be gifted to provide more than one service for your products and that is very good. However, when it comes to editing and proofreading, it is a good idea to have at least two individuals with the required skills to do these tasks so that your products will be of quality.

Communicating and Arranging Project Update Meetings

When working on projects or hiring additional tutors, you will need to get in the practice of communicating with your help. Therefore, here are some questions to get you started on planning out your meetings:

1. How often would you need to communicate changes?

   _____
   _____
   _____
   _____
   _____
   _____

2. How do you feel about email communication?

   _____
   _____
   _____
   _____
   _____
   _____

3. How will you manage physical meetings, conference calls, or virtual meetings?

_____
_____
_____
_____
_____

4. How will you hold contractors accountable for their work and communication?

_____
_____
_____
_____
_____

5. Will you send meeting schedules in advanced? Why or why not?

_____
_____
_____
_____
_____

6. What is your response time policy?

_____
_____
_____
_____
_____

Each of these questions will need to be answered so that you can get an idea of how you want to arrange project update meetings.

Expert's Advice:

Whether you are working on individual projects or a series of tutoring assignments, you will need to have a plan in place because there will be a lot of tasks that will be addressed as contractors begin working on their project. For example, there may be a content question that will need to be answered prior to moving on to the next phase. This is where your response policy comes in handy. The longer you take to respond, the longer the project takes, which can be very frustrating on both parties. However, mutual respect and understanding can go a long ways when it comes to working with others.

Now, I want you to understand how to set up project update meetings. Below are some guidelines to help you with that piece of the puzzle:

1. **Establish a Communication Schedule:** This can simply mean that you will check-in with prospective contractors every two weeks and tutors on a monthly schedule. If there is a project in progress, you should request that the contractor send a status update weekly or every two to three days to keep you informed of the project. The bottom line is that you need to be hands-on with your help, but not a micromanager. Let's face it...no one wants or excels under micromanagement.

2. **Use Electronic or Written Communication:** By communicating in writing, either electronically or traditional writing, it will save a lot of confusion and provide concrete evidence that documents the life of a project, including tutoring assignments. Therefore, I suggest that you use email to communicate so that you can keep a paper trail of what's happening. When it comes to project updates, they should definitely be written, preferably via email so that the message can be sent to more than one person whom is assigned to the project. Not to mention, email allows for immediate responses so projects will not

be delayed. Last but not least, if the need arises for court evidence regarding a project (let's hope not!), the documentation will be there.

3. **Use Conference Call Lines or Other Recording Services:** In the event that you need to speak verbally, you want to use voice systems that can be recorded so that you can manage and check in on project managers and tutors or other help. This gives everyone a chance to go back and listen to the presentation for future guidance.

4. **Limit Meetings:** Don't waste your time or contractor's time! This is not a good sign of success and contractors will resent that. It's already enough when they have to respond to emails or other requests daily. Keep in mind that they are running a business too and often have various valued clients, like you. In other words, please be cognizant of this reality. Besides, would you want to attend meetings that could have been emailed?

5. **Seek Input About Availability:** It is very common to think about your own availability, but you should also think about your team's availability. The best way to address this potential concern is to send out a survey to poll the team's availability. This will save you time with individual emails, but most importantly, it will provide everyone a chance to have their voice heard and feel like a team.

These five guidelines will definitely reduce stress for you and promote a sense of organization amongst the team. For sample project update emails, you can join our group at www.becomingabettertutor.com. There are a lot of resources available to help you with your tutoring business organizational needs.

Various Types of Validity and Reliability Measures

As you already know, tutoring is a challenge within itself. You do not need individuals questioning how you figured out the type of instructional plan that is necessary for their child. Similarly, if you happen to work with school districts, then you definitely want to justify how the learner's instructional plan was created, as you want to provide data-driven tutoring instruction. In a nutshell, you want to make sure that you are providing your clients with assessments that are both reliable and valid.

There are many types of validity and reliability measures that can be used in education. To make it easy for you, below are the most common types of validity and reliability measures:

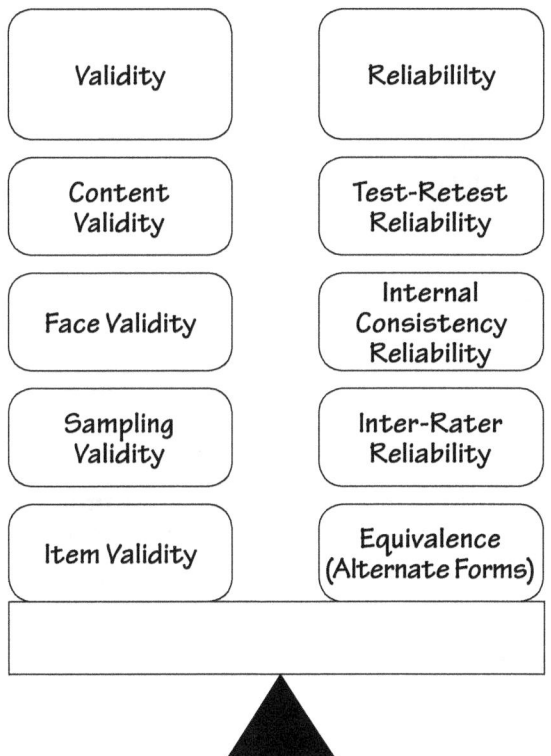

First, let's take a look at the various types of validity measures.

Content Validity

Content validity is the degree in which a test measures an intended content area. Content validity requires for both item validity and sampling validity (Gay & Airasian, 2003, p. 136). In other words, content validity is needed to ensure that the test is measuring what the student was taught and is supposed to learn.

Item and Sampling Validity

When it comes to item validity, it focuses on making sure that the assessment items are related to the actual content. In terms of sampling validity, this type of validity focuses on whether there is an equal amount of questions covering certain learning objectives. Imagine being tutored in math, when it comes time to take an assessment, you discover that the test is in science. This is where content validity comes in. Another example pertains to purchasing assessments. Imagine purchasing an assessment from an educational company. You discover that they advertised an assessment that covers five different learning objectives, but it only shows one learning objective. Do you think this assessment has good content validity? Why or why not?

Face Validity

There's another type of validity that is sometimes used in conjunction with content validity—face validity. You may be wondering what this type of validity means, but the truth is, the words speak for themselves. According to Gay and Airasian (2003), "While determining face validity is not a psychometrically sound way of estimating validity, the process is sometimes used as an initial screening procedure in test selection. It should be followed up by content validation" (p. 137). In other words, face validity must be triangulated by using content validity. As the old saying goes, "If it looks like a dog, it must be a dog." Unfortunately, this is not always true when it comes to face validity. It is best to always follow-up with content validity to ensure the test measures tutoring with learning objectives outlined in the learner's instructional plan.

Now, let's take a look at the various types of reliability.

Test-Retest Reliability

This type of reliability is the degree to which scores on the same test are consistent over time (Gay & Airasian, 2003, p. 142). This means that the same test is given at one specific time should be the same or close to the same when the test is being re-administered. In tutoring, this type of reliability is very important because students are tested multiple times throughout their tutoring program.

Internal Consistency Reliability

This type of reliability focuses on one test at a time. "Because internal consistency approaches require only one test administration, sources of measurement errors, such as differences in testing conditions, are eliminated" (Gay & Airasian, 2003, p. 143). In other words, there are not multiple testing conditions that can cause an increase in errors. In tutoring, this is very important because most learners take their own assessments in an individual setting. In order to determine reliability, individuals must use a statistical formula.

Inter-rater Reliability

The scorer/rater reliability is used with essay tests, short-answer tests, performance and product tests, projective tests, and observations—almost any test that calls for more than a one-word response (Gay & Airasian, 2003, p. 145). In other words, if the test is not multiple choices, then it should undergo the scorer/rater reliability to determine if the results are reliable.

In tutoring, this is very important because tutors may decide to give essay prompts to assess the learner's knowledge. Please know that essay items can be used in all content areas. A great way to use this method is during a content meeting with tutors to help them better understand how important your tutoring company value quality assessments.

Equivalence (Alternate Forms)

Equivalence is similar, but do not have the same items on the test. According to Gay and Airasian (2003), "Equivalence exists when the two forms measure the same variable, have the same number of items, the same structure, the same difficulty level, and the same directions for administration, scoring, and interpretation" (p. 142). In other words, this is when more than one assessment of the same form is being used to assess student achievement. In tutoring, this is very important because learning organizations will need to have multiple forms regarding content, especially if they serve a large population.

Below are some questions to help you establish validity and reliability for your products:

1. Do you plan on selling curriculum products such as student workbooks? Why or why not?

   _____
   _____
   _____
   _____
   _____

2. What are your experiences with designing assessments?

   _____
   _____
   _____
   _____
   _____

3. Have you planned out how you will establish validity and reliability? What is your plan?

   _____
   _____

4. How much manpower do you have to support curriculum projects?

5. In your own words, describe the impact that reliability and validity will have own your learning organization.

These five questions will definitely help you plan, but most importantly, they will help you realize why you need to understand and provide tutoring products and assessments that have been deemed both reliable and valid.

Gay and Airasian (2003) say it best, "All test scores have some degree of measurement error, and the smaller the amount of error, the more reliable the scores and the more confidence we have in the consistency and stability of test takers' performances" (p. 141). The bottom line is that no test is perfect, but there are measures that can be taken to ensure that test scores are deemed both valid and reliable.

> **Expert's Advice:**
> The best advice that I can give regarding both validity and reliability is to purchase a good educational research textbook that breaks it down for you. Personally, I think that type of book should be in your professional library anyway. As you will quickly find out, there is always something to learn about in the world of educational assessments.

In this chapter, you had a chance to develop a quality control plan for your tutoring business. Most importantly, you have some strategies to help you provide data-driven instruction by making sure that assessments are deemed both valid and reliable and being in tune with how to develop a plan to provide both quality products and services.

You now have read the blueprint to get started. Let your spirit guide you in making the right decisions when protecting your learning organization.

Where to Go From Here

Look out for other Dr. Alicia Holland-Johnson's products. You can join our group at www.becomingabettertutor.com to gain exclusive content, reserve either group or personal tutor coaching sessions, network with like-minded tutors, and stay updated about various aspects of the tutoring industry.

Should you have questions or comments for Dr. Holland-Johnson, suggestions for future material, or tips, feel free to email her at drhollandj@becomingabettertutor.com. Don't forget to check out a great premium tutoring resource at www.becomingabettertutor.com.

Until next time, Happy Tutoring!

CHAPTER 9

Implementing Quality Assurance Meetings

Depending on where you are with hiring other staff, it will depend on the type of meetings on which you will need to have to ensure that quality assurance occurs in your process to deliver quality products and services. In this chapter, we will explore a variety of meetings that may be necessary to implement within your learning organization. These meetings are the following:

- Informational Meetings
- Operational Meetings
- Brainstorming Meetings
- Kick-Off Meetings
- Strategic Meetings

Informational Meetings

The first type of meeting that you should plan are informational meetings. Those type of meetings require for you and your leadership team to inform attendees about specific challenges, concerns and new insights that may impact a project. In your own professional experiences, you may have attended a staff meeting, informational or interest meeting to get more information going.

Informational meetings should be held at least one a month. Whether it is face-to-face or online. If you are planning on having an online meeting, then you would need to figure out how to go about it. If you feel that it is necessary to host information on your company's intranet, then it may make sense to share information that way and you will know that it is secured.

Operational Meetings

The second type of meetings in which you should hold are operational meetings. These types of meetings could be considered informational, but it would be for your leadership team. It is at this meeting where each department share what is going on, in which, a department head or director would share this information.

Operational meetings are also good for communicating the master meeting schedule for any board leadership, staff, specialization meetings and so forth. Below are some questions to help you reflect open areas that you may want to implement at your operational meetings:

1. How do you plan for your staff to provide a program updates?
   _____
   _____
   _____
   _____
   _____

2. What specific guidelines would you have in place for your staff to follow in operational meetings or meetings in general?

3. What kind of information would you be sharing with the staff?

4. How do you plan on addressing any challenges, questions, needs, and other comments that may come up during the meeting?

5. How would you communicate any budgetary changes?

6. How do you plan on discussing next steps with staff?
_____
_____
_____
_____
_____
_____

7. How would you communicate who is on the leadership team?
_____
_____
_____
_____
_____
_____

This are just some question to help you get started with your operational meetings.

Brainstorming Meetings

The third type of meetings that you would need to consider are brainstorming meetings. These types of meeting are extremely important because they spark the creativity that provides the innovation that is necessary to keep you as the company who provides both quality products and services.

It is important to understand that Brainstorming meetings should serve these two purposes:

> Ideas should be generated without interruption of addressing how it will be done.

> Gather each person's ideas after they have had the time to meditate on the task.

This is not the meeting to take action because no action is necessary at this point. Staff and the leadership team are having opportunities to hear their voice be heard and provide an avenue to include all staff and leaders that are associated with a particular project.

Kick-Off Meetings

The fourth type of meeting that you would need to consider are kick-off meetings. These types of meetings are used to get everyone acquainted with the project, especially with project deliverables, and key staff that will be participating in the meeting.

Below are some questions to help you plan your kick-off meetings:

1. What would be in your welcome email to kick-off the project?

   _____
   _____
   _____
   _____
   _____

2. What would be the suggested meeting days and times, including time zones for the project?

   _____
   _____
   _____
   _____
   _____

3. What would be the agenda for this type of meetings?

   _____
   _____
   _____
   _____

4. Who is responsible for the agenda?

5. What platform are you using to host your meetings?

6. Will they be face-to-face, phone, or online meetings? Why or why not?

7. Will these meetings be recorded? Why or why not?

8. What type of pre-work would you address, if any, is necessary?

_____
_____
_____
_____
_____

9. How do you plan on having each member introduce himself or herself?

_____
_____
_____
_____
_____

10. How do you plan on incorporating next steps into the meetings?

_____
_____
_____
_____
_____

This are just some question to help you get started with your kick-off meetings.

Strategic Meetings

The fifth type of meeting in which I would like to discuss are Strategic meetings. In these type of meetings, a group consensus is needed to help formulate the plan to carry out the strategy. These types of meetings should be held at least once or twice a month to allow for leadership to implement the strategy. For example, a new strategy is implemented one week. The group consensus is to report back in two weeks with specific data to measure the progress and/or effectiveness of the strategy. That way, at the next strategic meetings, there will be new information to discuss and could plan the next steps as a team.

1. How do you plan for your staff to provide a program updates?

2. What specific guidelines would you have in place for your staff to follow in operational meetings or meetings in general?

3. What kind of information would you be sharing with the staff?

4. How do you plan on addressing any challenges, questions, needs, and other comments that may come up during the meeting?

_____
_____
_____
_____
_____
_____

5. How would you communicate any budgetary changes?

_____
_____
_____
_____
_____
_____

6. How do you plan on discussing next steps with staff?

_____
_____
_____
_____
_____
_____

7. How would you communicate who is on the leadership team?

_____
_____
_____
_____
_____
_____

These are just some questions to help you get started with your strategic meetings.

CHAPTER 10

Creating an Online Project Management System for your Content Team

When you start working with multiple subject matter experts, staff, and employees, you are going to learn very quickly that you need a system to help you track what everyone is doing and a system for you to keep up with all the projects as you plan them. In this chapter, we are going to look at some reflective questions to help you as you plan your own online project management system.

The first step though is to focus on the following questions as the leader:

Questions for You, The Leader

1. Why do I need an online project management system?
2. What is an appropriate timeframe to plan, design, and implement this system within our learning organization?
3. How much resources do I need to allocate to ensure that the budget for this project is within our budget approval?

Now, let's look at some of the questions in which you should ask yourself about designing your organization's project management platform.

These questions are the following:

1. How do you plan on adding a functionality to include assigning multiple projects for multiple staff?

   _____
   _____
   _____
   _____
   _____

2. Will you add start/end dates and status functionalities for these projects? Why or Why not?

   _____
   _____
   _____
   _____
   _____

3. How do you plan on keeping track of discussions related to each project within the system?

   _____
   _____
   _____
   _____
   _____

4. How do you plan on incorporating to-do lists into this system?

   _____
   _____
   _____
   _____
   _____

5. Will you be able to add files associated with each project within the system? Why or Why not?

   _____
   _____
   _____
   _____
   _____

6. How do you plan to incorporate a calendar lecture into the project system?

   _____
   _____
   _____
   _____
   _____

7. How do you plan on managing tasks and task comments?

   _____
   _____
   _____
   _____
   _____

8. How do you plan on measuring each project's progress?

_____
_____
_____
_____
_____

9. How do you plan on documenting each employee and staff member's performance?

_____
_____
_____
_____
_____

10. What are the specific metrics that you will use?

_____
_____
_____
_____
_____

11. What type of reports would you be interested in generating for each staff or staff meetings?

_____
_____
_____
_____
_____

12. What type of reports would you be interested in generating for the leadership team?

_____
_____
_____
_____
_____
_____

13. Would you want to send messages automatically? Why or Why not?

_____
_____
_____
_____
_____
_____

14. What type of features do you plan on implementing to help with quality assurance?

_____
_____
_____
_____
_____
_____

15. How do you feel about implementing an internal messaging system dedicated only to projects?

_____
_____
_____
_____
_____
_____

16. How do you plan on assigning appropriate permissions within the system?

_____
_____
_____
_____
_____

These questions and your responses to these questions should help you come up with functionalities that will support you in designing your own online platform for project management. As you are answering these questions and another question comes up that you need assistance with, then please email me and let me know. Perhaps, I could share some more food for thought questions for you.

Dr. Holland's Advice

After you have designed your project management platform, it is important to create a handbook with screenshots that will help your staff navigate through the site so that everyone can be productive.

This chapter was designed only to help you reflect on your project management needs. I hope that you found the reflection questions helpful to you.

Part IV:
Conducting Research in Your Learning Organization

CHAPTER 11

Implementing Focus Groups & Market Research

You are at a point now in your business where you need feedback from people who understands that thou opinion matters. Whether you are planning on developing a new product or service, it is important to gain feedback from individuals who are not emotionally attached to the both the process and the outcome. AT some point in your own life, you may have participated in some type of questionnaire or survey that solicited your opinion about a particular product or service. In this chapter, we are going to discuss how to implement focus groups and conduct market research for your own learning organization.

Why Focus Groups?

Focus groups are designed to get a qualitative snapshot from a small group of diverse people, usually 5-15 people. For instance, if you are trying to get feedback about how your tutoring services should be designed for special needs learners, then you would want to have a small group that understands from multiple perspectives. Here's a visual og how that might look:

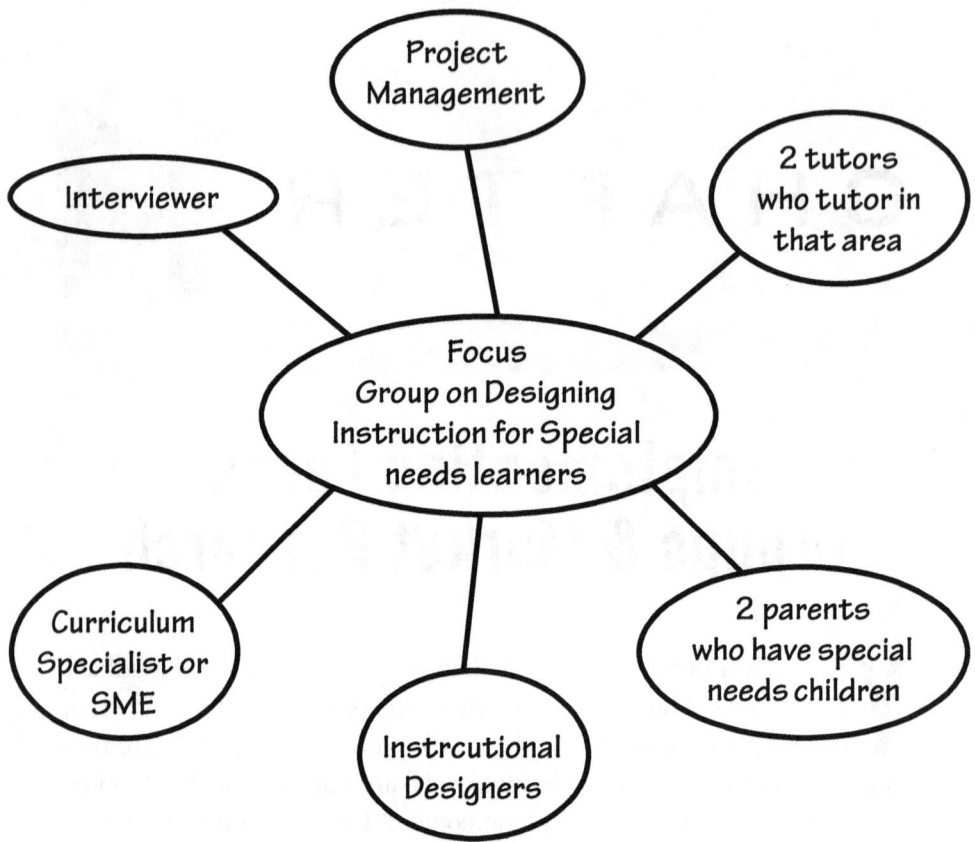

In this visual, you may have noticed that there are two tutors participating in the focus group because they actually tutor students who have special needs. Therefore, their perspectives, attitudes, beliefs and opinions are extremely important to help better understand the tutoring process. Another participant you may notice is that there is a subject matter Expert or Curriculum Specialist included in this focus group. His or her perspective affords the opportunity to zone in on the content to ensure that the content is developed at industry standard, but could discuss ways to modify or enhance the content with visuals and other graphic organizers. A third participant is the instructional designer who is focused on formatting the lessons in a sequence that makes sense for the learners. Two other participants are the parents of special need children. They know their child better than anyone else so it is important to have their voice included in this particular focus group.

The last two participants include both the project manager and interviewer. While the project manager may not be included in the actual designs of the lessons, but his or her role is to keep the project moving forward. In terms of the interviewer, this individual is familiar with the research aspect of the process and does not have any emotional attachment to the project. Therefore, this helps with validating the results from the focus group.

As you can imagine, focus groups are very important and should be a part of your research process in your learning organization.

How to Implement Focus Group

When it comes time to implement focus groups within your learning organization, it is important to consider a few questions. Below are some reflective questions that will help you implement and run your focus group with ease:

1. How do you plan on having the discussions recorded?

   _____
   _____
   _____
   _____
   _____

2. How do you plan on organizing the data collected from these discussions?

   _____
   _____

3. How many participants do you plan to have in your focus group?

4. What are the criteria that will be used to select participants to join the focus group?

5. What type of questions would you ask during the focus group?

6. How long do you think the focus group should last? Please allocate time per question to be realistic?

7. What process would you use to invite participants to your focus group?

8. How would you explain the purpose of the focus groups?

9. How would you explain how issues of confidentiality will be dealt with?

10. What are the expectations for the facilitator?

11. What are the selection process for a facilitator?

12. What materials and resources would be needed to prepare for the focus group?

13. What are the actions steps for leaders who have conducted the focus group?

These are some questions that will help guide you to implementing focus group into your learning organization.

What is Market Research?

Market research is a form of research that you can use to understand how a particular market may be performing as it relates to products and services. Also, market research can be used to solve problems, obtain information on competitors, and what other information is necessary to stay in the competitive market. Some examples of these marketing research efforts include focus groups, one-one-one interviews, test marketing, or phone surveys. In this chapter, we are only focusing on focus groups, but let's start with the basics of marketing research.

Why Market Research?

Market Research is the foundation of how you plan to offer innovative solutions to your clients. It's something that should not be taken lightly and you would need to figure out how to have a team dedicated to this ongoing initiative. Let's look at scenarios that can help you see the value of market research:

> **Scenario: That's just what I am Looking For...**
> **Thank you Jesus!!**
>
> Kameran Kalender, a tutor business owner, had a vision while she was working out. The vision she had was to create a line of workbooks that catered to English teachers. This vision prompted her to do a simple Google Search that lasted for about 1 hour. It was at that time that she decided to follow through with the vision. It took about six months for her to bring the product to market. Kameran sent out a press release about the release and about the three days, she saw book sales soar by 30%. This trend continues for the next three months and that's when she realized that she made the right decision and decided to follow her vision.

Reflection

1. How do you feel about Kameran's decision to bring the product to market based upon her vision?

   _____
   _____
   _____
   _____
   _____

2. How do you monitor your own visions as a business owner?

   _____
   _____
   _____
   _____
   _____

3. What is your plan of action for implementing market research into your learning organization?

   _____
   _____
   _____
   _____
   _____

Scenario: I Can't Believe This!

Chance Collins, a well-respected leader in the tutoring community in his state, decided that he would bring to market a resume service for Adult English Language Learners, while he had a few clients who used his service, he was not able to grow his practice. His traffic for

> this particular service declined by 10% and the numbers continued to drop. After doing a search online, he later learned that there were 10 other business offering this service for free. There was no way that people would pay him for those services.

Reflection:

1. How do you feel about Chance Collin's decision?

2. What would have been your recommendation to him about conducting market research?

3. How can you avoid this in your own learning organization?

Dr. Holland's Advice:

These are two different scenarios to help better understand the importance of market research.

It can either work for you or against you if not utilized. The bottom line is that market research is very important in business when it comes to offering innovative products and services.

CHAPTER 12

Disseminating Your Research for Your Learning Organization

You may be at a point in your tutoring career that things are going well and you want to start sharing knowledge with like-minded professionals. In this chapter, we are going to look at several ways to disseminate your research for your learning organization.

Conferences	Academic Journals
Books	In-House

Staying In-House

The first avenue for disseminating your research would be in your own learning organization. This gives you the confidence that you need and a chance to get feedback from an audience that is familiar with the topic in which you are presenting. You need to make sure that you administer a survey to get their feedback. Depending on the learning organization, it will depend on the type of research that will be shared. Typically, it will be action research that can better assist tutor practitioners on how to use data-driven practices.

Presenting at Conferences

The second avenue for disseminating your research would be at conferences that fit your target audience. Conferences are great avenues to network and meet likeminded professionals. When you plan to present, you want to make sure that the conference benefits you and has a good reputation.

Creating Physical and Digital Resources

Depending on your professional aspirations, there are opportunities for you to write about what you know. This is something that you will need to plan out and be strategic about it. Types of books in which you may decide to include in your learning organization:

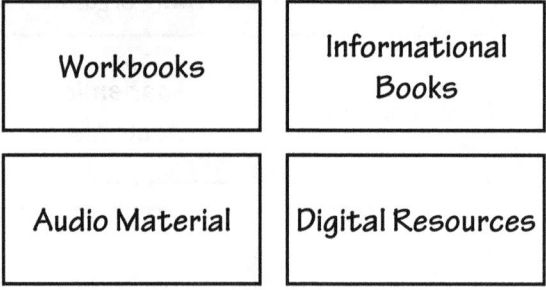

Physical Resources for Clients

The first type of resources are workbooks. You may decide that your clients would benefit from customized lessons and extra practice. Depending on what you tutor, you would develop materials around those topics.

The second type of resources are books. You may decide that you want to include a library of literature that would supplement their existing program. You could hire writers that specialize in children's literature or another genre that would benefit your clients.

Digital Resources for Clients

You may opt to make some of these physical resources available as digital resources. You may also decide to design resources that are exclusively for digital learning.

Dr. Holland's Advice

You will discover quickly which resources would be better suited as either physical or digital. This is something only you can decide and it should be bases upon the client's needs. IF you are developing physical and digital products, then you need to protect them. At a minimum, you should copyright everything. Remember the moment you write it down, it belongs to you since you are the creator. I am not a lawyer, so please consult a legal expert that specialize in intellectual property law.

Scenario: Wait...When Did I Give You Permission to Use My Stuff!!

Will King, a business and statistics tutor, created a series of signature workbooks. He did not want to digitalize these workbooks just yet because he was hosting most of his workshops live. He found an online publisher that catered to self-publishing and began producing multiple copies. One day Will went online and decided to google his name, along with his company's products. He got very upset because he had found his intellectual property on an online streaming service. He did not authorize anyone to post his work online and later discovered that people could download his work for free. He contacted the company and reported a copyright infringement and they immediately took care of the situation after he provided legal documentation that he was authorized to act on behalf of the company.

Reflection:

What is your plan to protect your or your company's intellectual property in the digital world?

_____
_____
_____
_____
_____

Getting Published in an Academic Journal

When you work makes it in an academic journal, this is when prestige and accolades come along with this professional and public achievement. You want to make sure that you are able to have copyright of your work, along with the publisher so that you can have control of your work. Typically, academic and/or scholarly works consist of research studies, case studies, critical book reviews, and academic chapter, you will need to make sense of the type of scholarly work in which you would like to publish for betterment of the tutoring industry.

Dr. Holland's Advice

As in International Researcher and Practitioner, I have experienced a great deal of research studies in both qualitative and quantitative. There is a system in place called the Cabell's to help researchers and practitioner find suitable targeted journals to submit their academic works. This is a god place to start. However, the landscape of Scholarly publishing has changed and the entry to barrier is not as grand as it used to be. Therefore, you have to be careful of predatory publishers. There will be some publishers who charge a free if your article is accepted, while others would do it for free. You will have to decide which option is best for your work. There is a list that trials to help with identifying predatory publishers called Beall's List, but it appears that the list has been forced to be removed from the Internet. From my experiences, I have seen a good ethical research that needs to be disseminated to the masses get rejected for publication. Why? The peer reviewers didn't understand the content, there was not enough "statistical" difference, or the topic was not of interest to the journal. The bottom line is make sure that you do good ethical research and find a targeted journal that is of quality and has a rigorous peer review process. At the end of the day, your research ends up at the same place so make sure that your work is indexed so people can find it from all over the world. Happy Researching!

If you need support in this area, then I am available for a coaching session. You can reach me at support@thetutoroutreach.com to request a session with me.

Where to Go From Here

Look out for other Dr. Alicia Holland's products and services. You can stay updated by visiting her personal website, www.dr-holland.com. You can also contact her via the contact form on her personal website to request services.

Should you have questions or comments, suggestions for future material, or tips, feel free to email her at: drhollandj@thetutoroutreach.com.

Join our Membership Group

Visit www.expandyourtutoringbusinessblog.com to gain access to exclusive content and interact with Dr. Alicia Holland so that you can strategically move your tutoring business from good to great.

Last but not least, if you are interested in networking with like-minded tutor business owners, join our FREE Closed Facebook Group—Expand Your Tutoring Business.

Our Closed Facebook Group is growing fast and group members are eager to connect with you and share their tutoring experiences with you. We truly have what you would call a Professional Learning Community.

Until next time, Happy Tutoring!

About the Author

Dr. Alicia Holland is one of those rare people who can say she is an educator, professional tutor, instructional designer, curriculum developer, online professor, life coach, consultant, speaker, and author and mean it. She started her teaching career at the age of 20 and later earned her doctorate degree in Education from Nova Southeastern University in Ft. Lauderdale, Florida in 2010 at the age of 26. Her God-Given talents and skills have attracted clients such as school districts throughout the United States, state agencies, and other leading learning organizations, including in the private sector.

Dr. Holland consults with tutors and other learning organizations both large and small. Her tutoring blog for tutors has been online since 2010 and she coaches tutors around the world. Typically, she speaks at major conferences each year on topics in education, including tutoring. Dr. Holland is an online associate faculty member at Concordia University Portland where she teaches doctoral level organizational leadership and writing courses in the School of Education.

Also, Dr. Holland has held appointments as an online professor at Ashford University, American College of Education, and Everest Online where she served in the capacity of Internship Supervisor for Bilingual and English Language Learner Educators and taught various courses in Education, Life Skills and Critical Thinking. Additionally, at Capella University, in the Graduate School of Education, she taught various courses in Education and currently serves as a Dissertation Mentor for Doctoral Learners. Lastly, Dr. Holland teaches doctoral level research courses and serve as either Dissertation Chair or Committee Member at the University of Phoenix. Currently, she is serving as a Lead Area Faculty Chair in Research and was awarded and recognized as one of the 2016 Research Fellows for her research on *Meditation, Mindfulness, and Critical Thinking*. In July 2017, Dr. Holland and her research team will present the original research at Ryerson University in Toronto, Canada.

Outside of Academia, Dr. Holland is a Transformational, Intuitive Life Coach and Ordained Spiritual Minister. In September 2016, she presented her personal development presentation, *Changing Your Client's Story through Personal Power* at Harvard University in Boston, Massachusetts. In November 2017, Dr. Alise will be in Paris, France (City of Love & Freedom) sharing research on *"Integrating Flower Essences Therapy and Intuition in Life Coaching"* at the 8th International Conference on Traditional & Alternative Medicine.

When Dr. Holland is not developing new content, life coaching, tutoring, teaching, or consulting with her clients, you can usually find her sight-seeing and spending quality time with her family enjoying the Desert Sunrises and Sunsets.

References

EEO.gov (2012). Equal Employment Opportunity is the law. Retrieved June 4, 2012, from http://www.eeoc.gov/employers/upload/eeoc_self_print_poster.pdf

Gay, L. R. & Airasian, P. (2003). Educational research: Competencies for analysis and applications. Upper Saddle River, NJ: Merrill Prentice Hall.

Merriam-Webster Online Dictionary (2012). Definition of copyright. Retrieved June 2, 2012, from http://www.merriamwebster.com/dictionary/copyright?show=0&t=1337553301

Merriam-Webster Online Dictionary (2012). Definition of intellectual property. Retrieved June 2, 2012, from http://www.merriamwebster.com/dictionary/intellectual%20property

Merriam-Webster Online Dictionary (2012). Definition of patent. Retrieved June 2, 2012, from http://www.merriam-webster.com/dictionary/patent

Merriam-Webster Online Dictionary (2010). Definition of trademark. Retrieved June 2, 2012, from http://www.merriamwebster.com/dictionary/trademark

Nanus, B. (1992). Visionary leadership: Creating a compelling sense of direction for your organization. San Francisco: Jossey-Bass

U.S. Department of Education (2011). Bringing flexibility and focus to education law: Looking back and moving forward. Retrieved June 12, 2012, from http://www.ed.gov/sites/default/files/looking-back-moving-forward.pdf

Index

A

Age Discrimination in Employment Act (ADEA) of 1967, 37–38
Agreements, 6–17
    confidentiality and non-disclosure agreements, 14–15
    license agreements, 16–17
    non-compete agreements, 9–11
    project agreements, 11–14
    tutor agreements, 7–9
    types of, 6–15
    work-for-hire agreements, 6–7
Americans with Disabilities Act (ADA) of 1990, 38
Assessments of student progress, 49–50
    validity and reliability measures, 65–70
Attorneys, hiring, 4, 5
Authors of content-related projects, 59–60

B

Business plans, 19–35
    components, 23–24
    financial analysis, 33–34
    management plan, 31–33
    market analysis, 27–29
    necessity of, 20–23
    office operations, 25–27
    products and services, 24–25
    sales strategy, 30–31
    self-funding and, 21–22
    Supplemental Educational Services (SES) approval and, 22–23
    supporting documents, 34

C

Civil Rights Act of 1964, 38
Communications
    project updates, 61–64
    schedules, 63
Compensation of employees and contractors, 32–33
Conference calls, 64
Confidentiality agreements, 14–15
Content development, 59–60
    authors, 59–60
    contractors, 59–61
    editors, 57
    graphic designers, 59–60
    indexers, 59–60
    review process, 59–61
    validity and reliability measures, 65–70
Contractors
    communication schedule, 63
    confidentiality and non-disclosure agreements, 14–15
    content development projects, 59–61
    management plan, 32–33
    meetings with, 64
    project agreements, 11–14
    project update communications, 63–64
    work-for-hire agreements, 6–7
Copyrights, 2–4
    defined, 2
    registering, 2–3, 5–6
    trade secrets and, 4–5
    tutoring business materials, 3
Curriculum development
    confidentiality and non-disclosure agreements, 14–15
    project agreements, 11–14
    validity and reliability measures, 65–70
    writers and editors, 57–59

D

Data collection in tutoring sessions
    instructional learning plans, 49
    mini-assessments, 50
    monitoring notes, 48
    overview, 47

pre- and post-assessments, 49
progress monitoring assessments, 50
progress reports, 49
Data-driven strategies
business plans, 19–35
quality control plans, 53–70
validity and reliability measures, 65–70
Definitions
copyrights, 2
intellectual property, 1
patents, 2
trademarks, 2
Disabled clients or employees, ADA requirements, 38
Disabled persons, ADA provisions, 38
Discrimination prohibitions under federal laws, 37–38

E
Editors
content-related projects, 59–60
curriculum development, 57–59
test items, 57
Electronic communications, 63–64
Elementary and Secondary Education Act (ESEA), 36
Employees
federal employment laws. *See* **Federal laws.**
management plan, 32–33
organizational chart, 57
tutors. *See* **Tutors.**
work agreements. *See* **Work agreements.**
Employees' rights protection plans, 41–42
Equal Employment Opportunity (EEO), 37
Equivalent forms of assessment, 68
ESEA (Elementary and Secondary Education Act), 36

F
Face validity, 66–67
Family Educational Rights and Privacy Act (FERPA), 36–37
Federal laws, 35–38
Age Discrimination in Employment Act (ADEA) of 1967, 37–38
Americans with Disabilities Act (ADA) of 1990, 38
Civil Rights Act of 1964, 38
Elementary and Secondary Education Act (ESEA), 36

Equal Employment Opportunity (EEO), 37
Family Educational Rights and Privacy Act (FERPA), 36–37
No Child Left Behind (NCLB) Act, 22, 36
Financial analysis, business plan, 33–34
Freelancers. *See* **Contractors**

G

Government work
federal laws, 35–38
labeling proprietary information, 5
SES tutor providers, 22–23, 36, 47
student health and safety plans, 47
Graphic designers of content-related projects, 59–60

H

Health and safety plans for students, 42–47

I

Independent contractors. *See* **Contractors**
Indexers of content-related products, 59–60
Industry market analysis, 27–29
Instructional learning plans, 49
Intellectual property, 1–17
confidentiality and non-disclosure agreements, 14–15
copyrights, 2–4
defined, 1
licensing products, 16–17
logos and taglines, 4
records of, 15
trade secrets, 4–5
types of, 1–6
Internal consistency reliability, 67
Inter-rater reliability, 67–68
Item and sampling validity, 66

K

Key employees, management plan, 32–33

L

Laws. *See* **Federal laws**

Lawyers, hiring, 4, 5
Licensing products, 16–17
Logos and taglines, 4

M

Management plans, 31–33
Market analysis, 27–29
Marketing strategy, 30–31
Meetings, communicating and arranging, 61–64
Mini-assessments, 50
Monitoring notes, 48

N

No Child Left Behind (NCLB) Act, 22, 36
Non-compete agreements, 9–11
Non-disclosure agreements, 14–15

O

Office operations plan, 25–27
Older employees, ADEA requirements, 37–38
Organizational charts, 56–59

P

Patents, 2, 5–6
Products
    business plans, 24–25
    content-related, 59–61
    curriculum development. *See* **Curriculum development.**
    licensing, 16–17
    review process, 59–61
    validity and reliability measures, 65–70
Progress of student, documenting, 47–51
Progress reports, 49
Project manager, 57
Projects
    agreements, 11–14
    confidentiality and non-disclosure agreements, 14–15
    content-related products, 59–61
    meetings, communicating and arranging, 61–64
    updates, communicating, 61–64
Proofreaders of written products, 59–60

Q

Qualitative and quantitative data on student progress, 48–50
Quality control plans, 53–70
    components, 53–54
    meetings, communicating and arranging, 61–64
    organizational chart, 56–59
    questions to consider, 54–56
    validity and reliability measures, 65–70

R

Recordkeeping
    access by students and parents under FERPA, 36–37
    intellectual property records, 15
    student progress, 47–51
Reliability measures, 65–70
Rights protection plans, 38–42
    employees, 41–42
    safeguards, 42
    students, 39–41

S

Safety and health plans for students, 42–47
Sales strategy, 30–31
Sampling validity, 66
Self-funding the business, 21–22
Services
    business plans, 24–25
    products. *See* **Products.**
    review process, 59–61
SES (Supplemental Educational Services)
   tutor providers, 22–23, 36, 47
Start-up costs, business plan, 33–34
Student Health and Safety Plans, 42–47
Student progress, documenting, 47–51
Students' Rights Protection Plans, 39–41
Supplemental Educational Services (SES)
   tutor providers, 22–23, 36, 47

T

Taglines and logos, 4
Test items, writers and editors, 57
Test-retest reliability, 67
Trade secrets, 4–5
    confidentiality and non-disclosure agreements, 14–15
Trademarks, 2
Tutor agreements, 7–9
Tutors
    communication schedule, 63
    confidentiality and non-disclosure agreements, 14–15
    non-compete agreements, 9–11

V

Validity and reliability measures, 65–70
    alternate forms, 68
    content validity, 66
    equivalence, 68
    face validity, 66–67
    internal consistency reliability, 67
    inter-rater reliability, 67–68
    item and sampling validity, 66
    questions to consider, 68–70
    test-retest reliability, 67
    types, 65–66
Vision of company, 20–21, 33

W

Work agreements, 6–15
    confidentiality and non-disclosure agreements, 14–15
    non-compete agreements, 9–11
    project agreements, 11–14
    tutor agreements, 7–9
    types of, 6–15
    work-for-hire agreements, 6–7
Work-for-hire agreements, 6–7
Writers
    content-related projects, 59–60
    curriculum development, 57–59
    of test items, 57
Written communications, 63–64

www.ingramcontent.com/pod-product-compliance
Lightning Source LLC
Chambersburg PA
CBHW070556160426
43199CB00014B/2523